"Far and away the best prize that life has to offer is the chance to work hard at work worth doing."

- **Theodore Roosevelt**

Printed in the United States of America

ISBN: 097459881X
Library of Congress Control Number: 2003115931

Cover design: Salvatore Concialdi
Book Consultant/Editor: Paula Bermont

Bermont, Todd, 1964-
        10 Insider Secrets™ Career Transition Workshop/
Todd Bermont - - 2nd Ed.

10 INSIDER SECRETS™
CAREER TRANSITION WORKSHOP

Your complete guide to discovering the *ideal* job!

SPECIAL EDITION
NEW & IMPROVED!

Written by:
Todd Bermont

Author of:
10 Insider Secrets to a Winning Job Search
10 Insider Secrets to Job Hunting Success
Cognitive Selling™

10 STEP
Publications

CHICAGO

Todd L. Bermont
President
10 Step Corporation
(888) 894-6400
tbermont@10stepjobsearch.com

> *"Look at a day when you are supremely satisfied at the end. It's not a day when you lounge around doing nothing; it's when you've had everything to do, and you've done it."*
>
> **- Margaret Thatcher**

DEDICATION

This book is dedicated to my lovely and wonderful wife Paula. Her love and support provide me with daily inspiration.

> *"A journey of a thousand miles begins with a single step."*
>
> **- Chinese Proverb**

ACKNOWLEDGEMENTS

I am deeply grateful to everyone who has helped me in the preparation of this manuscript. Thank you to Harold Bermont, Caryn Cialkowski, Paula Bermont and Wendy Bonadio.

I would also like to thank the following individuals for their tremendous support and encouragement: Jeff Meyer, Andrew Pultman, Kenneth Weine, Chuck Goding, Nathaniel Bermont, Eric Bermont and Debbie Bermont.

In addition, I would like to thank my previous employers for providing me with a foundation for success: Royal Dutch Shell Corporation, NCR Corporation, IBM Corporation, American Power Conversion, and the University of Chicago's Graham School of General Studies.

Finally, I would like to thank each of you, the readers, for your confidence in me, in this workshop, and in your own ability to succeed.

> *"The path to success is to take massive, determined action."*
>
> **- Anthony Robbins**

CONTENTS

PART I: EXPLORING YOUR ESSENCE

"A mediocre idea that generates enthusiasm will go further than a great idea that inspires no one."

- Mary Kay Ash

INTRODUCTION

Welcome to the second edition of *10 Insider Secrets™ Career Transition Workshop* by Todd Bermont. This exciting and interactive workshop is designed to help you find the job of your dreams. If you are in the process of looking for your first job… or, if you dislike your current job… or, if you are out of work and want a new direction… this workshop is written for you.

For many people, money alone is not enough. Some want to feel a sense of purpose, to add value to society, or to regain balance in their lives. Others want to have a career that is fun and rewarding. If you are going through life feeling that something is missing… or believing that there should be more to your life than what you are living, you will appreciate this workshop.

You spend almost half of your life working. When you are unhappy in your work, it negatively impacts the other areas of your life.

Often, we can become frustrated or depressed when we are not living our lives in synchronization with our purpose, our values and our passions. The key is to find joy, happiness and fulfillment in what we do.

To be delighted with your career and your life, you must know what motivates you. To truly succeed, as Anthony Robbins would say, you have to *"live with passion!"* By the time you complete this workshop you will have the foundation necessary to identify your ideal career; one you can look forward to each and every day.

Once you determine your ideal job, the rest is easy. After this book, if you want more help, you can find a complete guide to getting the job you want in the book ***10 Insider Secrets to a Winning Job Search*** by Todd Bermont.

For now, let's focus on discovering the career of your dreams. Do not skip any chapters. Some may seem trivial and at times redundant. However, I can assure you that everything in this workshop is essential.

Together, we will walk through a step-by-step process to finding your ideal job. I designed this book to be an interactive workshop, as if you are attending your own, personal, career coaching session with me.

Normally, career coaching can cost as much as $250 per hour. I created this workshop so you can achieve similar results for a fraction of the cost.

While reading this book, try to imagine me coaching you one-on-one, in person. Typically in a coaching session, I sit at a desk or table across from my client and ask the very same questions that I will ask you in this workshop.

Each time I ask you a question, imagine that you are sitting on the other side of the desk from me, for your own personal coaching session. Answer each question with the same urgency as if you were actually paying $250 an hour to do this.

I will describe to you 10 secrets to finding career satisfaction. Like a funnel, at first, we will gather lots of information. Then, we will methodically sift through what is gathered to narrow your focus down to what you really want to do for a living.

After each secret, I will ask you some very personal questions. Answer each question as completely as you can. In doing so, you will get the most value out of the time we spend together.

Thank you so much for investing your hard-earned time and money in this career transition workshop. Let's begin.

SECRET #1:
PERSONAL REFLECTION

The first secret to any successful career transition is to learn about you. By gaining insight into your being and your essence, you begin to build the foundation for successfully determining your ideal career.

Have you ever asked yourself questions like *"Who are you?"* or *"What do you really want in life?"* Often, our lives are so hectic that we can get caught up in the moment and miss the big picture. We forget to take a step back to really learn about ourselves.

When was the last time you went on a first date? Do you remember that date? What did you do on that date? If you are anything like me, you probably tried to find out as much about the other person as you could. On my first dates, I asked questions about interests, hobbies, values, job and family background.

Now… when was the last time you asked yourself about your interests, values, etc.? It's so easy to take ourselves for granted. We rarely offer ourselves the same courtesy that we do for others. Sometimes the best way to understand our being is to pretend we are going on a first date with ourselves, to discover what makes us tick.

Just like you need to learn all about another person to have a successful relationship, you too need to know as much as possible about yourself … to make an educated career decision.

Imagine trying to buy a suit for someone you don't know. Is the person tall or short, stout or skinny, trendy or traditional? When you have no idea what this person looks like or what style is preferred, how likely are you to pick out a suit that will please that person? I doubt you would have much success.

Determining your ideal job is the same. If you don't know what motivates you, or what your interests are, how are you going to find the job of your dreams? Throughout this workshop, I am going to provide you with questions I want you to ask yourself, to help you focus on what you *really* want to do for a living.

However, don't just limit yourself to the questions I ask. Feel free to ask yourself other questions and to go more in-depth. The more you can learn about yourself and your desires now, the better your chances will be of selecting a career that you can be truly passionate about and enjoy.

How would your best friend describe you?

We view ourselves in one respect, but others often view us differently. This question allows you to view yourself from a perspective that you might not otherwise see. Once you identify who you are, you will be able to have a much better idea of what types of jobs you can and should seek.

For example, if you describe yourself as competitive, people-oriented and outgoing, then sales may be a great career for you. If instead you are detail-oriented, technical, and process-oriented then network management or software programming may be a better fit for you. If you are creative and free-spirited, perhaps you might enjoy graphic design or architecture. Get the picture?

If, I asked your friend to describe you, what would he or she say? After you answer this question, you may want to actually call some of your best friends and ask them. Their responses may surprise you. Getting a perspective from others will be helpful as other people will be judging you throughout your job search. It's better to know, now, if there are areas you need to address, rather than during the interview process.

How would your best friend describe you?
(Personality, ambition, hobbies, interests, knowledge...)

_____

_____

_____

_____

_____

_____

_____

_____

_____

_____

_____

_____

_____

What gives you the most joy in life?

Now that you have described yourself from the eyes of someone else, you have established the starting point on your journey to finding the ideal job. Later in the journey, you'll look back to this question when brainstorming on all of your possibilities. The next step is to look at what provides you with the most joy in life.

Joy can come in different shapes and forms. Family and balance may provide the most joy for some. While others may dervive satisfaction and self-worth by how much they make or their job title. Many define joy by spirituality and living out one's life purpose. Still, others find joy in solving tough problems or being a team leader. By understanding what gives you true pleasure, you will be better able to determine what you should do for a living.

"I hate my job!" - How many times have you heard someone say that?

One of the biggest reasons why people dislike their careers is that they are doing something that just "pays the bills" rather than doing something truly enjoyable and fun. Also, people often sacrifice balance in life to achieve success on the job. That lack of balance many times leads to frustrations, misery and regret.

I can't think of a single person who, when faced with death, said *"Wow... I wish I had worked harder."* Instead, I have heard things like *"I wish I had enjoyed life more... I wish I had spent more time with my children and family... I wish I had traveled more when I was younger... etc."*

To find a career you can be passionate about, look for jobs that provide you with many of the things in life that give you joy. It sounds so simple, yet it's so easy to neglect our joy. Ideally, you want to find a job that offers you many of the qualities and characteristics that you like with very few traits that you dislike.

Sometimes, it's that easy!

What gives you the most joy in life?
(Recognition, family, money, challenge, sports, competition...)

_____

_____

_____

_____

_____

_____

_____

_____

_____

_____

_____

_____

_____

What you are most grateful for in your life?

In life, it is so easy to focus on the negative. Negativity is everywhere. Turn on the evening news or pick up a local newspaper and most of what you hear and see are negative stories and events. In fact, let's see if I can predict what will be on your local news tonight. Hmmm... a murder... a bombing... a public health issue... a traffic accident... a bad economic report... or some sort of world crisis.

With all of the terrible stuff that can happen in the world, it's no wonder we focus on the negative. However, this is the absolute worst thing you can do if you want a life of happiness and joy. Negativity is like a nasty storm cloud hanging over your head. Negativity causes frustration, depression, and a lack of productivity. Negativity can also dampen and prolong a job search. You are what you think. Think positive!

Focus on the good in life

Rather than falling in a trap of negativity, it is so much more productive to focus on the positive. When you purposely look to the good, your subconscious mind is free as a butterfly and invites in all sorts of positive energy.

When you take the time to ponder and list what you are thankful for, you will feel better about your life and yourself. By identifying what it is you are grateful for, you can look for careers that can foster even more gratitude. One of the things I am grateful for is freedom. Throughout my career, I have always looked for jobs that allowed me the freedom to make most of the day-to-day decisions.

By starting each and every day with gratitude, you also gain an unintended benefit... you open up your energy flow to receive abundance and joy. While this may sound way out there... the Universe tends to reward gratitude. Gratitude tunes you into an energetic vibration that attracts positive energy. This positive energy brings about improved health, happiness and opens up doors to opportunities you may never have thought were possible.

What are you most grateful for in your life?
(Health, intelligence, wealth, education, friends, and family...)

_____

_____

_____

_____

_____

_____

_____

_____

_____

_____

_____

_____

_____

There is so much in life to be thankful for

The first time I put together a gratitude list, I was shocked at how truly blessed I have been. I immediately realized that my life wasn't so bad after all. I was downright happy to be me. I hope, after you listed some of the things you are grateful for, that you, too, experienced a similar high. Hopefully in completing this exercise, you are proud to be you!

What in your life causes you the most pain?

There's an old adage that says that if you had the choice of keeping your problems or taking someone else's, that once you truly understood everyone else's problems, you would wind up taking your own all over again. However, many have said that pain is stronger than pleasure. Often, we don't change until we have so much pain associated with a situation or circumstance that we are forced to change.

In your previous jobs, what has frustrated you the most?

You don't want to choose another job that will continue to further your pain. For instance, if you hate corporate politics and are tired of not being appreciated, this may be a result of you working for a large company. You might be able to rid yourself of this pain by working for an entrepreneurial company instead.

Often people put themselves in similar situations time and time again. Then, they wonder why they can't find a job they enjoy. They are quick to blame anyone and everyone except themselves.

You *do* have control over your career

You don't have to work in a job you hate. Identify what frustrates you so you can learn how to avoid it. Later in this workshop, as you begin to funnel out your ideal job, you'll want to look back at your answers to this question. Make sure any job you choose minimizes pain and maximizes pleasure.

What are you most frustrated about in your life?
(Debt, lack of passion, being overworked, no balance...)

_____

_____

_____

_____

_____

_____

_____

_____

_____

_____

_____

_____

_____

> *"You will find the key to success under the alarm clock."*
>
> **- Benjamin Franklin**

SECRET #2:
AWAKEN YOUR PASSION

Congratulations! You have just completed the first step to a successful career transition! You should now have a greater knowledge and appreciation of yourself. By identifying what you are most thankful for in your life, hopefully you feel encouraged and invigorated. Life is wonderful and should be cherished.

The next step in finding the job of your dreams is to identify your passions. Many people slump through life doing a job they can't stand just to pay the bills. Then, they wonder why they aren't happy and hate Mondays so much.

It is possible to love your career. But, to do so you must have passion for what you are doing. It is proven that when you are doing something you enjoy and are passionate about; you will be far more successful and make more money than otherwise. But, how do you know what careers you can truly be passionate about?

First you need to discover what it is that really excites you. In the following questions, I am going to ask you to describe your passions and ideals. Later, I will ask you to brainstorm the potential careers that can feed your passion.

"Live with passion!"

- Anthony Robbins

What are your greatest passions?

Passion is something that provides you with boundless enthusiasm. It's possible to be passionate about things as diverse as a hobby, a sport, a person, a task, or literally a million other things. The key is to find a job that fosters many of the things that you are passionate about.

For instance, if travel is one of your passions, you can find many jobs that will allow you to travel. Sales, training, speaking, consulting and meeting planning, are all careers you can choose, that will allow you to travel. If cooking is one of your passions, there are thousands of different jobs that can invigorate you... from chef to buyer to restaurant manager.

> *"I can tell you one thing. I've done this my way. I don't have anybody to blame for this win but me, and I love it.*
>
> **– John Daly**

What are your passions?
(Travel, work, cooking, sports, sharing stories, hobbies...)

_____

_____

_____

_____

_____

_____

_____

_____

_____

_____

_____

_____

_____

Do you know a person who has an ideal life?

Why would I ask this? Well, in the next question, I am going to ask you to describe *your* ideal life. Typically, when I ask that question, people have no idea where to start or how to answer that question. However, it is often easier to recognize the lifestyle you want when you see someone else living it.

For me, I respect the life of one particularly successful author, speaker and consultant. I won't name his name, but this person always seems to get the most out of life. He helps others and, in the process, does well physically, financially, and mentally. He travels the world and meets many great people.

However, you may have a totally different person you admire. If so, who is that person? How does that person live their life? What does that person do for a living? What experience did that person have to get to where they are? Can you replicate it?

If you set your mind to it, you have the ability to achieve almost anything. The key is to have the fire, the drive and the confidence to make it happen. There are millions of rags to riches stories out there. One of them could be yours! You just have to want it bad enough!

> *"Whoever said, 'It's not whether you win or lose that counts,' probably lost."*
>
> **– Martina Navratilova**

Do you know a person who has an ideal life? If so, who is that person and what makes their life ideal?

_____

_____

_____

_____

_____

_____

_____

_____

_____

_____

_____

_____

_____

Can you describe your ideal life?

For me, my ideal life is to be healthy, spiritual, balanced, financially stable, and happily employed, while sharing it with a family I love and living it with passion. What is yours? If you have no idea what an ideal life would be, how can you ever achieve true happiness? It's like playing darts blindfolded. If you are blindfolded, how likely are you to hit a bulls-eye?

To find happiness in life you have to know what will make you happy. I know it sounds so simple. However, if it is so easy, how come more people aren't happy? Just like in darts, you have to see your target before you can hit it. If you don't know what you want in life, it will be extremely difficult for you to achieve it.

If you had your ideal life, what would it be like? What would you want to be doing for a living?

If you are not sure what you want in life, then try the reverse. Whose life *wouldn't* you want to live? What things *don't* you want in your life? Sometimes it's easier to articulate what you *don't* want versus what you *do*. By identifying what you *don't* want, you can eliminate many potential careers. That will help you focus on finding the job you *do* want.

> *"I've missed more than 9000 shots in my career. I've lost almost 300 games. 26 times, I've been trusted to take the game winning shot and missed. I've failed over and over again in my life. And that is why I succeed."*
>
> **– Michael Jordan**

Describe your ideal life:

_____

_____

_____

_____

_____

_____

_____

_____

_____

_____

_____

_____

_____

> *"There is real magic in enthusiasm. It spells the difference between mediocrity and accomplishment."*
>
> **- Norman Vincent Peale**

SECRET #3:
EXPLORE YOUR VALUES & PURPOSE

Fantastic! You now have identified some of your passions and ideals. You are well on your way to a successful career transition. The next step is to review your values and purpose.

Often, on the surface, a job or career may seem rewarding. Perhaps you are making lots of money, or maybe you are doing something you are passionate about. Yet, with all of those things, you might still feel a sense of frustration or a lack of fulfillment.

When things seem great, yet you aren't happy, typically you are doing something that is not in alignment with your values and/or your purpose.

Money and passion are certainly important components to a rewarding career. However, they often pale in comparison to values and purpose. Your values and your purpose are the core of your essence.

Examples of values include:

- Honesty
- Hard-working
- Loving
- Perfectionist
- Direct
- Empathetic

- High integrity
- Consistency
- Altruistic
- Loyal
- Passionate
- Respectful

- Detail-oriented
- Focused
- Independent
- Team player
- Truthful
- Forthright

Values are the foundation of your existence

If you value honesty, love and charity, how would you feel if you ended up working as a lawyer and you had to defend someone whom you knew was guilty? You might not feel too good about yourself, regardless how much money you were making, right? Would any amount of money make you feel differently?

However, let's say *instead* of honesty, love and charity, you valued things like ambition, drive, success, money and prestige. If so, then maybe being a lawyer in that same situation might not be so bad. I am not here to pass judgement on what values are right or wrong. Only you know what your values are and which ones are most important to you.

What values are important to you?

This is one of the most important questions you can ask yourself. It is nearly impossible to succeed in, and have passion for, a career that goes against your core values. Conversely, when you find a job that is congruent with your values, often success flows freely and seemingly without much effort.

> *"Flaming enthusiasm, backed by horse sense and persistence, is the quality that most frequently makes for success."*
>
> **– Dale Carnegie**

List and then rank your top values:
(Honesty, giving, consistency, loving, hardworking, respectful...)

_____

_____

_____

_____

_____

_____

_____

_____

_____

_____

_____

_____

_____

What do you enjoy most in life?

Suppose family, free time and work/life balance are things you appreciate most in life. What if you are working in a job where you are required to travel extensively? What if you have to work long hours? No matter how much money you are making, you might not be happy. However, if expensive cars and lavish dinners provide you with the most joy in life, a job that requires you to travel and work long hours may be okay for you.

The bottom line is to find a job that is in alignment with your most cherished values and a career that provides you with joy, fulfillment and happiness.

> *"A determined soul will do more with a rusty monkey wrench than a loafer will accomplish with all of the tools in a machine shop"*
>
> **– Robert Hughes**

What do you enjoy most in life?
(Family, money, freedom, driving, golf, sports, entertaining…)

_____

_____

_____

_____

_____

_____

_____

_____

_____

_____

_____

_____

What is your life's purpose?

Each of us was put on this Earth for a reason. Why are you here? What value are you supposed to add to the universe? Why is it that a baby can die just a couple of days after birth, yet someone else can live to be one hundred years old?

We are all here to serve a particular purpose. Some of us may never know what that purpose is. Purpose is one of life's greatest mysteries. Often, I think life would be so much easier if we were told why we are here and what we are supposed to accomplish. Unfortunately, it doesn't work that way. Our purpose is not written on our birth certificate. Wouldn't it be nice if it was?

While we may never know for sure what our life's purpose is, it is important to try to come up with at least some idea. I know I may seem to be getting too deep in this chapter. However, please stick with me on this one. I have seen far too many people who are unhappy due in great part to not living and working according to their values and purpose.

Purpose is the most elusive yet important component to our existence. Why were we put on this Earth? For me, I feel I was put on this Earth to motivate and help people, who want to succeed, to achieve their very best. That is why I enjoy writing, speaking, training and coaching.

We can often find clues to our purpose in our personality, our interests, our values, our friends and our life's experiences. Each of us has a different purpose. Each of us is a piece to the universe's puzzle. Without each and every one of us, the puzzle would not be complete.

For sports figures and celebrities, their purpose may be to entertain and bring joy to people. For doctors, their purpose may be to save lives. A teacher's purpose might be to inspire and provide guidance to their students. Someone may choose to go into the Army to fight for freedom.

What do you think is your life's purpose?

Describe your life's purpose:

_____

_____

_____

_____

_____

_____

_____

_____

_____

_____

_____

_____

_____

PART II: LEARNING FROM YOUR PAST

"We can chart our future clearly and wisely only when we know the path which has led to the present."

- Adlai E. Stevenson

SECRET #4:
SUMMARIZE YOUR EXPERIENCES

Terrific! Now you have completed one of the most difficult steps of the career transition process, self-reflection. The next stage in your journey is to review your work history. By looking back at your previous jobs and other relevant experiences you can discover the key aspects you want in your ideal career, while also identifying those things to avoid.

As you go through the next several questions, pretend you are being asked these questions in a job interview. Stick to relevant information. However, be honest with yourself. The purpose of this section is not to pass judgement on your past, but instead to learn from it.

First, I am going to ask you to summarize your most recent jobs and work experience. If you have never worked before, then try to focus on courses you have taken, volunteer work, or other life experiences like social clubs, sports teams, school, etc.

Next, I am going to ask you specific questions about what you liked and disliked about those experiences. Finally, we'll take a look into what motivates and de-motivates you.

The goal of this chapter is to look back at your past to get direction for the future. Life is like driving. For the most part we want to be looking forward. However, we need that rearview mirror to make sure we are moving forward safely and nothing from behind us is going to distract or harm us.

Summarize your most recent and relevant work experience

What were your responsibilities? Which jobs utilized your true talents and strengths? What emotions did you feel in each of these positions? Who were your bosses? What did you think about these bosses? How big were the companies you worked for? What was the culture in those companies? Did you like or dislike that culture?

You may discover that a job you did years ago, while being somewhat entry-level, stimulated you more than a vice-president's position does today. If so, why is that? What caused those emotions? What was it that you really enjoyed?

In part, due to looking into the emotions I experienced during my previous positions, I was able to determine what I wanted to do today. One of the reasons I love what I do now is because my job incorporates so many of the good things I have experienced and cherished from the past.

In deciding what I wanted to do for a living, some of my thoughts included:

- *"I want to feel that same excitement of closing a deal that I experienced while working for IBM."*
- *"I want a similar instant gratification to what I got when I sold a TV or VCR at Alice in Videoland."*
- *"I want to experience, day in and day out, the kind of high I got from doing a sales training at APC."*

If you're have a tough time summarizing your work history, try to identify your top 10 moments that you have had working for someone else. If you can't think of 10 things from your work experience, then think of your life in general.

The key is to learn the past so you can get direction for your future. Now before moving on, summarize your most recent and relevant experiences. Try to capture some of your emotions you had during those experiences.

Summarize your most recent & relevant work experience:
(Likes, dislikes, successes, failures, emotions...)

_____

_____

_____

_____

_____

_____

_____

_____

_____

_____

_____

_____

_____

What was your most favorite job? Why?

Out of the jobs you just summarized, what was your favorite one and why? If you didn't enjoy any of your most recent positions, how about any of the other jobs you worked?

Oddly enough, one of my favorite jobs was back in high school, selling TVs and VCRs for a company called Alice in Videoland. Every time I sold a VCR or a TV, the store manager would take cash right out of the cash register and pay me an instant bonus, called a "spiff." I loved getting this immediate reward after each sale.

Ever since then, I have always looked for a job that had a similar kind of instant gratification.

To effectively choose a career you can cherish, it's important to understand the qualities and characteristics that you have liked about jobs in the past.

Some of you might think that there is nothing you have liked in the past. Well, if you fall in that category, think hard. There has to be something you liked? I've yet to meet a person that didn't have at least a couple of good aspects that they liked about a particular job or situation.

Let's say you liked being a teacher's assistant in college. Perhaps you enjoyed the thrill of helping others or the power of being in control. Whatever it was that you liked about that position, you could try to find that stimulation in other positions.

When articulating your favorite job, try to comprehend those elements that made it your favorite. Was it a boss who was really supportive? Did you have a motivating compensation plan? Did you like working for a big company? Did you like the benefits? Did you like your daily responsibilities? What was it that really made you enjoy that job?

What were your *most* favorite jobs? Why?

_____

_____

_____

_____

_____

_____

_____

_____

_____

_____

_____

_____

_____

What was your least favorite job? Why?

Now that you have summarized your most favorite jobs, I want you to write down what your least favorite positions were and why. This is just as important as the last exercise because you don't want to repeat the same career mistakes, or should I say learning experiences.

I always told my employees that if you make a mistake once, that is okay. A first mistake is a learning experience. It is when you repeat a mistake that it becomes a problem. The key is to learn from each of your situations. By identifying what jobs you did *not* like, and why, you can learn what causes you to dislike a job and make a conscious effort to avoid similar situations in the future.

For instance, if you dislike bureaucracy, and that was the reason you hated your last two jobs, then don't look for a new position in a large company. Most likely, you'll find the same bureaucracy in any large company. Instead, you may want to focus on small and mid-sized companies that are more entrepreneurial.

The job I hated the most was a job I had in college selling typewriter ribbons. The dilemma was how I was instructed to sell those ribbons. I was supposed to call potential customers and pretend that I was a shipping clerk. They wanted me to tell these people that I made a mistake and shipped a bunch of ribbons to a company near by. Then I was supposed to ask if I could reroute the ribbons to them at a "big discount."

That job went against my core values. I was brought up to be honest and to always tell the truth. Here, as a part of my job, I was supposed to consciously lie. Well, after three weeks, I couldn't take it anymore. I had to quit. From then on, I said to myself that I never wanted a job that went against my core beliefs.

Earlier on, I asked you to articulate your values. Have any of the jobs that you disliked in the past, gone against these values? What jobs did you hate the most? Why?

What were your *least* favorite jobs? Why?

_____

_____

_____

_____

_____

_____

_____

_____

_____

_____

_____

_____

_____

What motivates you the most?

Now that you know what you like and dislike, it's time to look more closely into your motivations behind those likes and dislikes.

Can you identify the qualities and characteristics that really motivate you? Take a look at the jobs you liked the most. Think about some of the things that motivated you. Was it is money and prestige? Or, did you thrive on challenges or an entrepreneurial environment?

Being human, each one of us gets motivated by different things. Doctors and nurses may be motivated by helping others... while athletes may be motivated by the thrill of victory and entertaining others. Musicians may be motivated by being able to make a statement and providing joy to others... while politicians may be motivated by power or a desire to make a difference.

I am not ashamed to say that I am motivated in part by money. However, I am even more motivated by the thrill of a sale, beating out tough competition, inspiring people to succeed, helping people achieve their dreams, and giving to those in need.

What motivates you the most?

"The difference between the impossible and the possible lies in a person's determination."

– Tommy Lasorda

What motivates you the most?
(Money, prestige, competition, power, charity, awards, success...)

_____

_____

_____

_____

_____

_____

_____

_____

_____

_____

_____

_____

Were you honest with yourself?

Don't worry about making judgements or having "politically correct" answers. For instance, there is nothing wrong about being motivated by money. When I hired salespeople, if in the interview they didn't say money was one of their motivators, I didn't hire them. I wanted salespeople that were hungry and greedy. When I motivated them with the right compensation plan they would sell as much as possible.

One of the reasons so many people hate their jobs is because they aren't motivated either by the position, the compensation plan, or their bosses.

What discourages you the most?

Now that we covered what motivates you the most, now it's time to look at what de-motivates you. When a job is filled with de-motivating elements, the workday becomes a chore and seems to drag on forever.

Some of the things that have discouraged me the most throughout my career are things like, politics, bureaucracy, too many rules, lack of gratitude, and de-motivating compensation plans. How about you, what things have discouraged you the most in your previous positions?

Again, be honest. As I mentioned before, you want to avoid repeating the same mistakes you might have made earlier on in your career.

> *"When you come to a fork in the road,
> take it!"*
>
> – Yogi Berra

What discourages you the most?
(Bureaucracy, politics, lack of autonomy, lack of support...)

_____

_____

_____

_____

_____

_____

_____

_____

_____

_____

_____

_____

_____

Who were your *most & least* favorite bosses? Why?

The final aspects to consider when learning from your past experiences is to look at your previous bosses (or teachers if you are just graduating). By reflecting on your most favorite and least favorite bosses, you can identify the traits you want in your future bosses… and those you would like to avoid. Who was your favorite boss? What qualities and characteristics made that person your favorite?

One of my favorite bosses was a boss I had at APC. He fostered a competitive, yet fun environment. He was always supportive of his employees and didn't hesitate to help us when necessary. He always let others know of our achievements and, when warranted, made sure to say what a great job we were doing and how much he appreciated our efforts.

Conversely, the boss I hated the most… was also at APC. By no coincidence this was also my final boss at APC. I disliked this person so much I decided it was better to quit than to remain employed. This person showed employees very little respect. He was more focused on politics than on doing the job right. He was more of a dictator than a team leader. And rarely did he ever show appreciation for a job well done.

To be happy on a job… not only do you have to like what you are doing and respect the company you work for… you have to like your boss as well. Otherwise you'll end up quitting or get fired.

In the end at APC, I still liked my job and still valued the company. I just couldn't stand the person I was working for. So, I decided to quit. In that case, I didn't have a choice of bosses. Due to a company re-organization I had to work for someone else.

However, you do have a choice. When changing jobs, you have the ultimate say on the person you will work for. As easy as it sounds… ideally you want to work for someone who has many of the traits that your favorite boss(s) had and fewer of the ones your least favorite boss(s).

Who was your *most* favorite boss? Why?

_____

_____

_____

_____

_____

_____

Who was your *least* favorite boss? Why?

_____

_____

_____

_____

_____

_____

> *"When you have a dream, you've got to grab it and never let go."*
>
> **- Carol Burnett**

SECRET #5:
QUANTIFY YOUR STRENGTHS

How are you feeling so far? Are you starting to get a better idea of what motivates you and what doesn't? Are you starting to get a few ideas about what you should do for a living? If not, that is okay. You are already halfway there. So far, you have taken a deep, introspective look into your personality, passions, likes and dislikes.

The next step in your journey is to take a personal inventory of your key selling points. Key selling points are what differentiate you from all the other people in the workforce. Once you decide on your ideal career, you need to sell yourself to get that job you want. Your key selling points are what will make a company want to hire you.

Key selling points are also extremely instrumental in *determining* your ideal career. Let's face it if you want to be a baseball player, but you have absolutely no athletic skills, what are the chances that you will land a job with a professional team? You'll only get frustrated if you try.

You have to be honest with yourself and focus on those areas in which you have some talent or expertise. For instance, if you have a gregarious and outgoing personality, there are many careers to choose from that could capitalize on this. You could go for sales, teaching, public speaking, public relations, hospitality management, meeting planning, comedy, theater and even politics.

However, if your personality is detail-oriented and technical, then perhaps accounting, programming, civil engineering, architecture, or science-related positions may be better.

What are your most marketable personality traits?

Are you outgoing or reserved? Are you competitive or a natural leader? Perhaps you are great "people" person. Maybe you are driven and focused. Be honest with yourself and identify those aspects of your personality you feel make you the most marketable. By marketable, I mean, what traits you think employers will want the most.

Everyone has aspects of their personality to be proud of. I am proud of my compassionate, yet competitive nature. I am also proud of my drive and ambition, my wish to help others and my philosophy of treating others the way I want to be treated. Finally, I am proud of my cravings to exceed expectations and my balance between gratitude and desire.

What aspects of your personality are you most proud of?

What makes you the most marketable?

"Winning has always meant much to me, but winning friends has meant the most."

– Babe Dirikson Zaharias

List your best personality traits:

(Outgoing, competitive, conscientious, compassion, drive...)

_____

_____

_____

_____

_____

_____

_____

_____

_____

_____

_____

_____

What are your most marketable *personal* accomplishments?

Often, in our personal lives we have had tremendous personal accomplishments. Some of us have volunteered to be a guest teacher at a public school or to be a "Big Brother" or "Sister." Others have helped raise money for their churches or synagogues.

What have you done in your personal life that has had a positive impact on others? If nothing comes to mind, think of significant individual achievements.

Someone once told me how proud she was because she proved her doctors wrong and learned to walk again after a major accident. That showed tremendous determination, drive and dedication. Social work, teaching, motivational speaking, psychology and writing are all fields she could consider as a result of her personal accomplishment of beating the odds and learning to walk again.

> *"People with goals succeed because they know where they are going"*
>
> **– Earl Nightingale**

List your best *personal* accomplishments:
(Charity, graduating with honors, service, volunteering...)

_____

_____

_____

_____

_____

_____

_____

_____

_____

_____

_____

_____

What are your most marketable *work-related* accomplishments?

If you have any work experience, I am sure you have had some great accomplishments along the way. Work accomplishments can come in many different varieties. A couple of examples are good reviews and company awards.

If you are in sales, examples of work-related accomplishments could be achieving quota or making the "President's Club." If you are in consulting, an accomplishment may be successfully managing a project under budget and ahead of schedule or saving a valued customer over $1 million with a creative company reorganization.

Maybe you were written up in an internal company publication. Perhaps you turned an irate customer into a happy one and helped the company maintain a profitable customer. Even getting a "thank you" email from your boss or client could also be a great accomplishment.

What are your most celebrated work accomplishments? What are you the most proud of? What have you achieved throughout your career? If you haven't worked, then what scholastic accomplishments are you most proud of? Try to think of accomplishments that are quantifiable and attractive to potential employers.

Maybe you helped save a company $150,000 through developing a new procurement process. Perhaps you helped a company maintain one of their best customers by solving a potentially volatile situation. Maybe you graduated with honors.

Interviewers expect you to have quantifiable work-related accomplishments. They want to know what they can expect from you. If you have won a corporate award or have gotten a great review... that is something a potential employer can feel good about.

What have you achieved that you are most proud of?

What are your most marketable work-related accomplishments?

List your best *work-related* accomplishments:
(Awards, reviews, making quota, a great review, saving $...)

_____

_____

_____

_____

_____

_____

_____

_____

_____

_____

_____

_____

_____

List your most marketable work experience

Pretend you meet a stranger in an elevator who has no clue about you or what you might have done in the past or your line of work. What would you say if this stranger asked you *"What do you do for a living?"* How would you explain your expertise, your background and expertise to that person in the short period of time you are in the elevator?

Consider the types of descriptions you would put in the section of your resume where you start the sentence "Responsible for..." Make sure you focus on those things that make you the most marketable and attractive to prospective companies.

For me, experience that makes me marketable are qualities like, selling, training, keynote speaking, business development, sales management, career development, hiring, mentoring, and coaching.

What is your most marketable experience? What do you know how to do well? Are you a great programmer? Or are you a terrific motivator? Maybe you are the best cost-cutter that ever walked on earth?

What do you do best?

> *"Men of genius are admired, men of wealth are envied, men of power are feared; but only men of character are trusted."*
>
> **– Alfred Adler**

List your most marketable work experience:

(Advertising, management, customer service, cold calling, project-leader, programming, designing...)

_____

_____

_____

_____

_____

_____

_____

_____

_____

_____

_____

_____

What are your credentials? What other things do you know?

In your course of study, have you received any certifications? Have you learned how to do things that aren't directly required for a particular job, yet can provide benefit? Even though you may be a technically oriented person who has a job as an engineer, if you know how also know how to sell, that could make you a very marketable commodity.

What knowledge and expertise have you gained from your education, career and life experiences? If you worked for a company in the Information Technology (IT) industry, and that employer paid for you to get certified in a particular area, this certification is a great credential and could help you land a more lucrative opportunity.

If you learned how to use spreadsheet, word processing and presentation software, this can also be valuable career knowledge, even if you have nothing to do with the IT industry. Whether you want to be a lawyer, accountant, salesperson, teacher, social worker, or even a fashion designer, having some basic computer skills can make you more appealing to prospective companies.

Don't just limit yourself to computer career knowledge.

Any topic you studied in school could be perceived as valuable. A public speaking course or a course on how to teach could be just as important. Even a gym class could be a potential selling point if it taught you how to be competitive and how to win.

Whether you worked in IT, or a completely different area, the point is that you have learned many things in your life that can be applicable to your future career. By articulating these things, you give yourself a broader array of tools in which to explore your ideal career.

You also make yourself more marketable.

List your most marketable career knowledge & credentials:
(Certificates, C++, research, thesis...)

_____

_____

_____

_____

_____

_____

_____

_____

_____

_____

_____

_____

What else makes you a great individual?

Have I forgotten to ask you about any of your key selling points? Review the topics I asked you about and ask yourself if you have any other key selling points that we did not cover. What other tangible or intangible aspects about yourself can you come up with that differentiate you from everyone else?

Why would someone want to hire you? What would they want to hire you to do?

What makes you unique?

Later on, when I ask you to identify your ideal job, your key selling points will play a major role in what vocations you can choose and your ability to win a job in your desired career. While it would be nice to wave a magic wand to instantly develop the traits and characteristics you need to succeed in a dream career, obviously, that is not possible.

You need to be realistic about what you can do.

There could be a big difference between what you *can* do and what you *want* to do. For me, I would love to be a pro football place kicker. Nothing could be better than kicking the game-winning kick in the Super Bowl. However, the reality is that I am not athletic. At my age, it would be a bit difficult to develop the skills necessary to become a pro football place kicker.

Does that mean I can't find a career that I can be passionate about? No. I have many talents outside of athletics. The key is to understand what those talents are and find the best career possible to leverage those talents. The same is true for you.

We all have unique selling points that differentiate ourselves from everyone else. By identifying your core strengths and competencies, you will know what jobs you can do, and how to position yourself, so companies will want to hire you.

What other strengths & competencies do you have that would make companies want to hire you?

_____

_____

_____

_____

_____

_____

_____

_____

_____

_____

_____

_____

_____

PART III: BUILDING YOUR FUTURE

"The most damaging phrase in the language is:
It's always been done that way."

- Rear Admiral Grace Hopper

SECRET #6:
BRAINSTORM THE POSSIBILITIES

Now you've reached the fun part of this workshop, the time where you can dream. You are about to begin what is called a brainstorming session. The rules of brainstorming are simple. Just write down anything that comes to your mind.

There is no one right or wrong answer. Write down anything and everything that pops into your mind. However, before you start, take some time to reflect on the answers you gave during the first five secrets of this career transition workshop. The reason I took you through these exercises was to stimulate a thought process that brings you to this point.

Hopefully, by now you realize that you have many more options than you might have thought. The brainstorm you are about to begin is the time to be creative and discover all of your possibilities. Don't just list ideal options, but *any* idea that comes to mind. Have some fun!

Soon, I am going to ask you to list the possible jobs you can do. Don't worry yet about what you *want* to do, instead, write everything you *can* do based on your personality, your capabilities, your passions and your experience. Later, I will ask you to refine this list into what you really want to do.

How many different possibilities do you think you can come up with?

Hopefully you can think of at least ten to twenty ideas. If you don't right away, then give it some more time. Remember the purpose of an initial brainstorming session is to identify all the possibilities, not to make judgement on what is right or wrong.

Consider all of your options

Don't worry about what others think you should do. The purpose of this brainstorm is for you to list everything you can do.

When I decided to leave my last job to start my own business, I went through a similar brainstorming session. I listed all of the jobs, with my talents and expertise that I could do. Below is a partial list of the options I came up with for myself.

1. Teacher
2. Author
3. Speaker
4. Salesperson
5. Sales manager
6. Career coach
7. Sales consultant
8. Real estate agent
9. Insurance agent
10. Day trader
11. Financial analyst
12. Stock broker
13. Investment consultant
14. Product manager
15. Procurement manager
16. Vice president of sales
17. Global account manager
18. Sports writer
19. Radio program host
20. Newspaper or Magazine columnist

What can you do?

I am sure you can come up with at least 10 to 20 careers you could choose from. Don't be shy. This is the time to shoot for the moon. You'll be able to get more refined later. Right now... have some fun... and come up with a list of jobs you could do.

Job brainstorm: (Accountant, teacher, manager, etc.)

1. _____

2. _____

3. _____

4. _____

5. _____

6. _____

7. _____

8. _____

9. _____

10. _____

11. _____

12. _____

13. _____

14. _____

15. _____

16. _____

17. _____

18. _____

19. _____

20. _____

What job(s) would be ideal for you?

Once you have completed the initial job brainstorm, the next step is to look at what you wrote and ask yourself "Out of all of these possibilities, what do I really *want* to do for a living?"

This is the beginning of the funneling process.

Look back to your answers from the first five secrets. Consider your passions, your values, your strengths and anything else you feel is important in this decision-making process. Review what is important to you… in your life… and in your career. Then, take that filter and revisit the brainstorm you just completed.

Out of your initial brainstorm, pick out strictly the job or jobs that you would most *want* to do for a living and summarize those on the following page. At this point of the process make sure you are selective. It is impossible to have a successful job search when there are twenty different careers you are willing to work. Pick out only those jobs that truly are exciting for you.

> *"Without goals, and plans to reach them, you are like a ship that has set sail with no destination."*
>
> – Fitzhugh Dodson

List your ideal job(s):

_____

_____

_____

_____

_____

_____

_____

_____

_____

_____

_____

_____

_____

Describe the qualities & characteristics of your ideal company

It is one thing to identify that you want to be an architect, a teacher, or a salesperson, but where do you want to work? If you chose to be a customer service manager, there are literally hundreds of thousands of companies you could target. But which companies interest you?

Often people are not happy with their jobs, not because they dislike their job, but because they don't like the company they are working for. Working for a company you are proud of... and one where you fit into the corporate culture... can be just as important, if not more so, than the job itself.

On the next page, I want you to brainstorm on your ideal company. What kind of qualities and characteristics would it have? Would it be a large, publicly traded firm or would it be a small entrepreneurial company? Would it be a growing company or one that has predictable earnings?

Again, write down anything that comes to your mind. Later in the workshop I will help you refine the process further. One way you can get ideas for your brainstorm is to look at what you liked and disliked about companies you have worked for in the past.

Traits I looked for in companies included: market-leader, aggressive, entrepreneurial, civic-oriented, financial stability, publicly traded, international, competitive, quality products and solid customer service.

What qualities and characteristics are important to you?

"You must have long term goals to keep you from being frustrated by short term failures."

– Charles C. Noble

Company brainstorm:
(Big, small, liberal, conservative, public, aggressive, private, entrepreneurial, civic oriented...)

_____

_____

_____

_____

_____

_____

_____

_____

_____

_____

_____

_____

Summarize your ideal company

Now… it is once again time to sift through your brainstorm and capture those nuggets that really matter to you. Out of your brainstorm on ideal company characteristics, what are some of the most important qualities for you? What are the makers and breakers?

Pick out the most important characteristics and summarize what your ideal company would be like.

> *"It's more important to do the right thing than to do things right."*
>
> – Peter Drucker

Summarize your ideal company:

_____

_____

_____

_____

_____

_____

_____

_____

_____

_____

_____

_____

What industries interest you the most?

Now you have completed the initial two brainstorming sessions. First, you identified all of the different kinds of jobs you *could* do and summarized which ones you really *want* to do. Then, you listed out and summarized the characteristics you want in an ideal company.

Next, I am going to ask you to brainstorm on the industry, or industries, that interest you the most.

During my senior year of college, I received six job offers... all in sales. I received offers from Maytag, Venture Stores, Royal Dutch Shell, NCR, US Steel, and Central Transport.

But, which company did I want to choose?

It was tough because the offers started at $18,000 per year and went up to $26,000 per year. *(I know... I know... Now, I am really showing my age.)*

Well, it boiled down to the industry. I actually accepted the lowest salary offer, NCR, because when I made that decision, the computer industry was the best place to be. At that time, it was the most exciting and had the greatest potential for growth and opportunity.

However, had I graduated fifteen or twenty years later, I might have chosen something like biotechnology or an industry having to do with homeland security instead.

Again, it is what you want... not what you think others want for you. On the next page, brainstorm on all the industries that interest you. Also, write down the characteristics that make each one appealing.

For me, the industries that still excite me the most are, IT, finance, real estate, anything related to food (because I love to eat), travel, hospitality and sports.

How about you... what industries would really interest you?

Industry brainstorm:

(IT, apparel, entertainment, hospitality, electronics, finance, retail, insurance, automotive, hospitality, travel...)

1. _____

2. _____

3. _____

4. _____

5. _____

6. _____

7. _____

8. _____

9. _____

10. _____

11. _____

12. _____

13. _____

14. _____

15. _____

Summarize your ideal industry

Now that you have identified all of the industries that interest you... next... I am going to ask you to summarize the ones that interest you the most. Depending on what industry or industries you choose to seek, you will need to emphasize and promote different aspects about you and your work experience. Whether on your resume or in an interview, you will need a customized message for each industry opportunity.

I always recommend to my clients that they create a customized resume for each and every industry they are interested in. If you are looking for a new job in the same industry... then perhaps a chronological resume might work fine for you. However, if you are looking to change industries, you may want to use a functional resume instead.

If you would like more information on how to customize your resumes and cover letters I recommend you purchase a copy of the job-hunting book *10 Insider Secrets to a Winning Job Search* by Todd Bermont.

Customizing your message can be difficult and time consuming. That is one of the reasons why it is so important to limit your scope to just a couple of industries that really interest you the most, and ones where you have the best chance of landing your ideal job.

With that being said, take a look at your list of ideal industries and try to narrow it down to three or less. Industries can be broad in scope. Information Technology (IT), for instance, can encompass everything from computers, to networking, to software, to consulting services, to disaster recovery.

Finance can be anything from banking to lending to investing to credit. Consumer goods include everything from personal hygiene to packaged food to cleaning supplies. So for each industry, also include the subcategories that you want to focus on.

Summarize your ideal industry(s):

1. _____

_____

_____

_____

_____

2. _____

_____

_____

_____

_____

3. _____

_____

_____

_____

_____

Describe the qualities and characteristics of your ideal boss

The final step in brainstorming the possibilities is to describe your ideal boss. If you are working for someone you can't stand, it is almost impossible for a job to be rewarding and enjoyable.

Certainly company culture and responsibilities are critical contributors to job satisfaction. However, if you don't like your boss… forget it!

You'll find that throughout your job search process, be it in your interviews or correspondence, you will be able to tell who you would enjoy working for and who you wouldn't want to work for, regardless of the money involved. The last thing you want to do is to accept a job just because it pays good money… even though you don't like the person who will be your boss.

I guarantee you if you don't like your boss… you will be miserable. Ultimately either you will have to quit or you will get fired. I can not emphasize enough the importance of deciding what kind of person you want to work for in advance of your job search.

Most people just settle for any job. As a result most people aren't happy with their jobs. You can find a dream job. But you can't settle. Having the right boss is one of the most important facets to job satisfaction.

> *"Who you are speaks so loudly, I can't hear what you are saying."*
>
> - Ralph Waldo Emerson

Describe the qualities & traits of your ideal boss:
(Supportive, appreciative, helpful, empowering, empathetic...)

_____

_____

_____

_____

_____

_____

_____

_____

_____

_____

_____

_____

_____

> *"Vision is the art of seeing the invisible."*
>
> **- Jonathan Swift**

SECRET #7:
REFINE & FUNNEL YOUR IDEAS

Congratulations! You just completed a brainstorm of possible jobs, companies, industries and bosses you can choose from. You also began to prioritize some of the most important aspects of each. Now, the next step is to continue to refine your brainstorm and funnel those ideas into a more tangible and specific focus.

I will warn you that some of this may seem redundant. However, repetition is one way to ensure you are on the right path. The next exercise I am going to give you is pretty simple. From your summary of ideal jobs, identify the three most desirable.

It is okay if you can only come up with one. That makes your focus even clearer. However, don't list more than three, because it will be very difficult for you to achieve what you really want if you can't narrow it down. You must be clear in your intentions.

List your top three ideal jobs:
(Accounting, product manager, teacher, programmer...)

1. _____

2. _____

3. _____

Next, from your brainstorm, what industries interested you the most? Often your passions can help drive your ideal industries. For instance, if you have a passion for sports, then industries such as sporting goods, professional sports and consumer goods might be possibilities.

Let's say you have identified customer service as your ideal job and that you have a tremendous passion for helping people who are sick. You could apply for customer service positions in hospitals, pharmaceutical companies, HMOs, etc. Try to figure out the industries that you can be passionate about. If you are fascinated by computers… and you love the Internet… then there are literally hundreds of positions you could have in the IT industry.

List your top three ideal industries:
(Finance, insurance, consumer goods, entertainment…)

1. _____

2. _____

3. _____

Now, let's revisit your ideal company characteristics. If you described your personality as independent and entrepreneurial, you may be very unhappy working for a big, structured & bureaucratic company. However, if you are looking for job security, and constant change makes you frustrated, then a big company could be ideal for you.

Again, company traits can be anything from a company's culture to whether or not it is publicly traded. If you want to work for a company where stock options are part of the compensation plan, then getting a job with a private company won't likely accomplish your objective. From your company brainstorm, as well as any other ideas that may have jumped into your head, list your most important company characteristics.

List your top five ideal company characteristics:
(Private vs. public, Fortune 500 vs. small/midsize company, liberal or conservative, high growth vs. turnaround...)

1. _____

2. _____

3. _____

4. _____

5. _____

The next step in our refining process is to take a look at where you want to be in the future. **Where do you want to be in five years?** You may be thinking to yourself, *"I've heard that question on a million interviews. Can't you think of anything more original than that?"*

Well, companies ask you that question for a reason. They want to understand your goals and motivations. They want to see if you are the right fit for their organization. It is very important to ask yourself where you want to be in five years.

Do you want to be a manager? Not everyone does. If you don't want to be a manager, then don't say you do. Managing people can be very stressful. While it has lots of prestige, it also comes with very long hours and lots of corporate politics. Once you get into a managerial position, you have to "kiss a lot of behinds" to stay there. For some people, that is no problem. For others, it is a big issue.

By the way, it is okay to want to do the same thing five years from now. When I worked for IBM, there were some people who were in sales... or systems engineering... their entire careers. And, you know what? They loved it. They knew what to expect each year, had a consistent income, and developed many good friends along the way.

List your ideal career path for the next five years:
(Field work, management, retirement, self-employment...)

Year 1) _____

Year 2) _____

Year 3) _____

Year 4) _____

Year 5) _____

Regardless of where you want to be, each possible job can have a totally different structure. You could go into accounting at one company and be part of a large team, while at another you might be the only accountant. You could work in a company that fosters creativity or one that sticks very much to the "letter of the law," so to speak. What kind of structure do you want?

Look back into the previous secrets where you identified the qualities and characteristics you liked about your previous jobs. What did you like most about them? What did you like least? Then, focus your answer on what you liked the most.

Describe your ideal job structure:

(Specific goals and objectives, autonomy, team environment, creative vs. detailed...)

_____

_____

_____

_____

_____

_____

_____

_____

_____

_____

_____

_____

_____

How many hours do you want to work?

Per Day:_____ Per Week:_____

Be honest with yourself. If you are young and you don't mind working long hours, fantastic! However, if you are like me and have reached middle age and you are looking for more balance in your life, then maybe you don't want to work so many hours anymore.

It is important to consider your desired work hours. For instance, in pharmaceutical sales, you may only work from 9 to 5 because that's when doctors are generally available. However, other sales jobs might require you to work 70 hours a week because you need to network and attend many functions after normal work hours.

Do you want to travel? If yes, how much?

Per Day:_____ Per Week:_____

Are you raising a family? If so, you may not want to have a job that requires travel. If not, then maybe you want to see the world and travel on the company's money. If you do want to travel, how much are you willing to do so? Where would you like to travel? Would you want a Midwest territory or a global territory? Depending on the job, you could have either.

What office environment do you want?

Work out of the home or at an office?_____

Work at a local office or a corporate headquarters?_____

Wear casual dress or formal business attire?_____

What other environmental aspects do you desire?_____

Often something as fundamental as the office environment can determine your satisfaction in a job. Some of us love working out of the home, while others thrive on the stimulation of being in a large office.

Those of you who want to move up the corporate ladder may want to focus on opportunities that are located in a large regional office or corporate headquarters where you can get quality "face time." Conversely, if you don't want to be under the spotlight and you want to have more autonomy, then working in a small office or out of the home may be more appealing.

Where do you want to work?

Do you want to live in a large city or small town?_____

Which cities or towns?_____

_____

Do you want to work close to home or are you okay with a long commute?

_____

_____

One of my friends quit her job just because of the long commute. She spent over three hours a day in traffic. As a result, she had tremendous stress and anguish. Even though she loved the job, she was miserable because of all the time she had to waste commuting.

You might enjoy driving and not mind a commute. After all, while driving, you can listen to audio books, make phone calls, or turn on the radio. If that is the case, then you can focus on other aspects of your ideal job. However, if you do mind commuting, then incorporate that into your decision-making process.

What are your compensation & benefit objectives?

Salary: _____

Bonus/commission: _____

Vacation time: _____

Insurance: _____

Retirement plan: _____

Miscellaneous: _____

_____

_____

_____

Of all the characteristics of a job, the one most likely to cause either satisfaction or dissatisfaction is *compensation*. How much money do you need to earn to be happy? Have you ever sat down and put together a budget of your spending?

If you had your ideal lifestyle, how much do you need to make? Some people can raise a family of four on $30,000 and still be happy. Others can't raise a family of four for under $300,000 per year. It all depends on your interests, your goals, your objectives and your lifestyle.

Other things to consider are benefits and perks. For example, if you want an advanced degree, some companies will help you pay for this while others won't. This can make a huge difference. Maybe the salary may not be as high, but if a company is willing to spend thousands of dollars on your education, you might be willing to accept a slightly lower salary.

What kind of boss do you want to work for?

_____

_____

_____

_____

_____

_____

_____

_____

_____

Have you worked for a tyrant or a mentor? Did your previous bosses overlook everything or did they give you complete autonomy? It is very important to identify the kind of boss you want to work for. Look back at your previous brainstorms to find the traits you thought were important.

As I said before, you can have the ideal company and the ideal job, but if your boss is a real jerk, your life is going to be miserable. Consider aspects like management style, personality, and even gender as well. Some people are just more comfortable working for a man than a woman or vice versa.

> *"The important thing is this: to be able at any moment to sacrifice what we are for what we could become."*
>
> **- Charles Du Bos**

SECRET #8:
DEVELOP A GAME PLAN

Okay… you are almost done! Now is the time to complete the funneling process and come up with a game plan for where you want to work next.

We have spent the last several chapters together reflecting on your personality, your experience, and your goals and objectives. Hopefully this has been an enlightening process and one that you have enjoyed. Now that you know *where* you want to go, you must develop a plan *how* you will get there.

When you take a road trip, you don't just jump in your car and hope to get to where you are going, do you? Of course you don't. You first map out your journey… identify the best routes… then you go.

To get your ideal job you will need to do the same. So, together, let's briefly map out the optimal route to your ideal job. For a more in-depth look at this process, you may want to read the job-hunting book by Todd Bermont called *10 Insider Secrets to a Winning Job Search.*

However, for now, the following questions will help you complete your funnel. Again, bear with me. Some of this may seem redundant, but it helps to keep all of your important information in one concise place so it is easy for you to reference it in the future.

Summarize your ideal jobs/job descriptions:
(Accountant, advertising account executive, network administrator, vice-president of manufacturing...)

1. _____

2. _____

3. _____

Summarize your ideal industry(s):
(Banking, textiles, consumer electronics, medical, retailing, IT...)

1. _____

2. _____

3. _____

Now, look at the ideal job(s) and ideal industry(s) you listed above. On the next page I want you to list all of the possible companies you *can* target. While doing this, take into consideration the *"ideal company"* qualities and characteristics you summarized earlier in this workshop.

For instance, if you want to develop software for a company in the finance industry, you could list companies like Citibank, Merrill Lynch, Chase Manhattan, etc. If you want to teach third grade students, list out all the possible school districts in the locations that interest you. You could choose from public or private schools... inner city or suburban.

Just because you want to be a computer programmer doesn't mean you have to work for a computer company. Or, just because you want to teach doesn't mean you even have to teach at a school. In fact many companies have internal training staffs. So look beyond the obvious and list out all of the possible companies you *can* target.

Company brainstorm: (IBM, AT&T, Hewlett-Packard, Shaw, Sony, Merck, Wal-Mart, Exxon, Maytag, Starbucks, etc.)

1. _____

2. _____

3. _____

4. _____

5. _____

6. _____

7. _____

8. _____

9. _____

10. _____

11. _____

12. _____

13. _____

14. _____

15. _____

16. _____

17. _____

18. _____

19. _____

20. _____

Now that you have developed a list of companies you *can* target, review your company brainstorm and see which you *want* to target. Determine how realistic it is to work at each possibility. Then, come up with a list of the top 10 companies you *really want* to focus your job searching efforts on. This will be your concentration for the immediate future.

Targeted company list:

1. _____

2. _____

3. _____

4. _____

5. _____

6. _____

7. _____

8. _____

9. _____

10. _____

Now that you know the job(s) you want and the company(s) you desire, you need to develop a game plan to land interviews at these companies, so you can get your dream job. On the following page, I am going to show you some basic steps you need to take to develop your game plan. Just like a football team has to have a game plan for each game, you too need a plan to have a successful job search and a rewarding career transition.

SAMPLE CAREER TRANSITION PLAN

1. Identify the job(s) you want.   <u>Completed</u>

2. Identify the companies you want to target.   <u>Completed</u>

3. Identify your key selling points.   <u>Completed</u>

4. Customize your resume.   _____

5. Justify why you should be hired.   _____

6. Practice answering why you want to change jobs. _____

7. Develop a script for cold calling & networking. _____

8. Market yourself through networking, etc.   _____

9. Contact recruiters.   _____

10. Visit targeted websites & determine whom to contact. _____

11. Call potential bosses for informational interviews. _____

12. Attend tradeshows in industries of interest.   _____

13. Call friends, family, etc. to identify opportunities. _____

14. Attend career fairs.   _____

15. Make five "cold" calls a day.   _____

The key is to have a plan

On the previous page, I showed you a sample game plan for making a successful career transition. There is no single right or wrong way to create a game plan. The only bad plan is no plan at all. Prior to beginning your career transition process, make sure you have a game plan.

At the end of this workshop, I will provide you with a page in which you can start to detail your game plan. Keep this workshop with you and make sure you are following your plan. By the way, your plan doesn't have to be "written in stone." You may want to create it on your computer or use pencil on the pages provided. Feel free to modify your plan when necessary.

Before I send you off to develop your plan and to begin your career transition, I want to briefly cover two final topics, creating a job mission statement and conducting a reality check.

> *"Goals determine what you are going to be."*
>
> **- Julius Erving**

SECRET #9:
CREATE A MISSION STATEMENT

Look at any company's annual report. One of the first things you will typically find is a corporate mission statement. A mission statement is what drives the focus of the entire company and its corporate culture. Everything an employee does should ideally relate in some way to the company's mission statement.

The most successful and best-focused companies are those that ingrain the mission statement into their employees' minds.

To really be successful in your transition, you too need to have a mission statement that is short, concrete and easy to articulate. It is this mission statement that will ultimately drive your focus and your success throughout your job search.

Here are two examples of personal mission statements:

"To sell computers for a small entrepreneurial company where I can travel and have autonomy."

"To obtain a human resources management position with a large firm in my home town."

Again, imagine being in an elevator. If you only had ten seconds to tell someone in that elevator what kind of job you want, what would you say? What do you want people to remember? This message is what you should include in your mission statement.

The ultimate purpose of your mission statement is to crystallize your job-hunting focus. Don't rush this step! Your mission statement is what will direct you in the days to come and it will have an impact on the rest of your career. So don't take it lightly.

As you finalize your mission statement, say it out loud. How does it sound? Does it feel right? Are you confident when you say it? Do you truly believe in your mission statement?

The success of your career transition will directly relate to how well you can articulate your mission and how closely you follow it. Now... before moving on... put together your personal job-hunting mission statement.

Create your personal mission statement:

_____

_____

_____

_____

_____

_____

> *"Champions aren't made in gyms.*
> *Champions are made from something*
> *they have deep inside them – a desire, a*
> *dream, a vision."*
>
> **– Muhammad Ali**

SECRET #10:
CONDUCT A REALITY CHECK

One final step I want to talk to you about is to get *objective* feedback on your mission statement and direction. A career transition can be an emotional time. It helps to get a reality check.

Try to talk with at least a couple of people who can be objective about your career decisions. Either bounce your mission statement off of your friends, or try family… or even your spiritual leaders. Ask them if they think your career direction is realistic. Take them through your decision-making process. Do a sanity check to make sure what you are about to embark on makes sense, and is achievable.

Before I left my job to start my own business, I asked several friends *"Am I doing the right thing or am I crazy?"* Many of my friends brought up important points I had to consider before I made my decision.

List three people you can ask about your ideal career:

1. _____

2. _____

3. _____

Did you list three people who can be *objective*? Will they give you honest feedback without being afraid to hurt your feelings? If someone is just going to humor you, it won't do you any good. You are at a very critical juncture in your life and you need to be as sure as possible that you are making the right decisions.

One of the most objective ways to see if you are on target is to have "informational" interviews. This is an interview where you don't ask for a job. Instead, you ask for an honest assessment to determine if someone with your skills, experience, and personality can succeed in a given position.

Certainly, an informational interview can also lead to an actual job opportunity. However, that isn't necessarily the intent.

To get information interviews, contact people who either would be in a position to hire you or be a potential coworker. For instance, if you identified software development as your ideal position, then contact software managers or programmers.

For informational interviews, don't contact anyone in Human Resources. Ironically, often they are not able to help you determine your suitability for a particular position. They usually focus on tangible things like experience rather than important intangibles like ambition, personality and motivation. Instead, focus on those people who could be a potential boss or coworkers.

List three people you can have informational interviews with… in your ideal career:

1. _____

2. _____

3. _____

SUMMARY

Congratulations, you made it! You've just completed what might be the most important exercise in your life – identifying the career of your dreams. Now that you have a great idea of what you want to do for a living, summarize your goals and objectives, embrace your mission and develop a plan to get that job of your dreams. Then, take action and work your plan.

Remember, in the back of this workshop, I have provided you with a page you can use to start to plan your career transition. By creating and following a game plan for your career transition you are destined to be successful.

Thank you so much for spending your hard-earned time and money on this career transition workshop. I hope you found it to be beneficial in determining what you *really* want to do for a living. The key is to know what you want. Only you can determine that. After all… if you don't know what you want… how are you ever going to get it?

I am confident you have the drive, the desire and the capability to live a life full of happiness and success. Having the right job is a great building block to a fulfilling and rewarding life. I know you can find it.

I wish you the best of luck in your endeavors! I know you will succeed!

"We will either find a way, or make one!"

– Hannibal

> *"If you can dream it, you can do it."*
>
> **- Walt Disney**

Career Transition Game Plan

Activity   **Target date of completion**

_____   _____

_____   _____

_____   _____

_____   _____

_____   _____

_____   _____

_____   _____

_____   _____

_____   _____

_____   _____

_____   _____

_____   _____

_____   _____

_____   _____

> *"I would rather regret what I did do than what I didn't do!"*
>
> **- Margot Bermont**

ABOUT THE AUTHOR

Todd Bermont, President of 10 Step Corporation, is an author, keynote speaker, executive career coach and sales trainer. He has over 20 years of global Fortune 500 experience. As a top-level manager, he has hired, trained, and motivated employees worldwide. He has also been featured on CNN, FOX, CareerBuilder & Monster.com.

Prior to founding 10 Step Corporation, Bermont worked in corporate sales and executive management for NCR, IBM, and American Power Conversion Corporation. Bermont has conducted business with over 250 Fortune 500 clients… in over 20 countries worldwide.

Job-hunting and other career-related courses by Todd Bermont have been offered at the University of Chicago's Graham School of General Studies, Vernon Hills and Libertyville High Schools in Illinois and online through hundreds of colleges and universities across the country. In addition, Bermont has served on the Leadership Committee for the University of Chicago's Graham School of General Studies.

If you liked this Career Transition Workshop and are interested in other products and services offered by Todd Bermont, feel free to visit (www.10StepJobSearch.com) or call **(888) 894-6400**.

Current books by Todd Bermont include:

- *10 Insider Secrets to a Winning Job Search*
- *10 Insider Secret™ Career Transition Workshop*
- *Cognitive Selling™*

Services offered by Todd Bermont include:

- Executive Career Coaching
- Keynote and Motivational Speaking
- Sales Training

www.ingramcontent.com/pod-product-compliance
Lightning Source LLC
LaVergne TN
LVHW081318060426
835509LV00015B/1576